# OKLAHOMA CITY

## THE WAY WE WERE

Historical Photographs from the Collection of *The Oklahoman*

1910s-1941

Mission Point Press

# Contents

Published by Mission Point Press
All rights reserved
Copyright © 2018, Oklahoma Publishing Company

Mission Point Press
Chandler Lake Books
2554 Chandler Road
Traverse City, MI 49696
www.MissionPointPress.com
www.ChandlerLakeBooks.com
Edited by Monroe Dodd

Printed in the U.S.A.
by Walsworth Publishing, Marceline, MO.
No part of this book may be reproduced, stored
in a retrieval system or transmitted in any
form or by any means, electronic, mechanical, photocopying, record-
ing or otherwise, without the prior consent of the publisher.

First edition
ISBN: 978-1-943995-52-3
Library of Congress Control Number: 2018932688

Photographs
Dust jacket/cover, front: Christmas shoppers downtown, mid-
December 1934; back (clockwise from top left): 1929 Oklahoma City
Indians Manager Al "Lefty" Leifield, Luna the elephant and Zoo
Director Leo Blondin, city's first oil well in 1928, steel worker build-
ing Civic Center in 1936, veterans in line for bonus bonds in 1936,
bumper car ride at Springlake Amusement Park, and (center) sorority
sisters on float in stockyards anniversary parade in 1935.
Page 1: Faces in the crowd at opening of the Midwest Theater, 1930.
Page 2: Santa Fe shows off its newest streamliner, 1939.
Page 4: Crowd at inaugural ball of Governor William H. "Alfalfa Bill"
Murray, 1931.
Page 6: "Tribute to Range Riders" on the lawn of the Capitol.

# Introduction

A few years ago, author Jack Shafer dug into the origins of one of the most famous quotes about the news business. Although widely credited to late *Washington Post* publisher Philip Graham, it was determined that an editorial writer with the paper, Alan Barth, was apparently the first to comment, "News is only the first rough draft of history."

And what a wonderful first draft it has been. *Oklahoma City: The Way We Were* is a fascinating look at how *The Oklahoman*'s photographers told the story of Oklahoma City's good times and bad times.

Residents were captured inventing, learning, working, creating, celebrating, mourning and at play. This is the rare book that goes beyond staged photos and snapshots of buildings and events. In these pages we see daily life as it was captured through the lens of some legendary *Oklahoman* photographers. These images and tens of thousands more are now available to the public through the Oklahoma Publishing Company Photography Collection at the Oklahoma Historical Society.

Here are photos that haven't been published in decades, and many caught me by surprise. Early on, readers are treated to the photos, illustrations and coverage given to a visit by famed aviator Charles Lindbergh. The excitement that surrounded that event foreshadowed the growing importance of aviation in building the city and bringing it into the jet age.

Oklahoma City residents came together quite a bit, whether while Christmas shopping, at the early movie palaces that dotted downtown, at Springlake Amusement Park, for various sporting events, or at attractions like the Oklahoma City Zoo and area lakes.

Rarely seen photos show the impact of the Great Depression with scores of people lined up for work, food and housing. Oklahoma City's will to overcome adversity is showcased throughout, whether it's the construction of a "civic center" in the depths of the Great Depression or the construction of affordable housing for the working class and impoverished families hoping to get jobs at the stockyards.

Legends like Will Rogers and Wiley Post are remembered, along with colorful characters like "Alfalfa" Bill Murray. Our ongoing love-hate relationship with the weather is shown, whether it be the dust storms of the Great Depression, tornados or snow.

*Oklahoma City: The Way We Were* tells a story of who we are and how we got here, and it hints at how our history still shapes us as the city continues into its second century.

Steve Lackmeyer
*Reporter for* The Oklahoman *and local historian*

Time and again in the decades after statehood, the people of Oklahoma City turned out in force to marvel at celebrities, to commemorate great occasions and to share the experience of living in one of America's newest and fastest-growing cities.

## Lucky Lindy

Shortly after completing his solo voyage across the Atlantic in *The Spirit of St. Louis*, Charles Lindbergh toured the country, promoting aviation and basking in praise. On September 28, 1927, only months after his famed flight, Lindbergh arrived in Oklahoma City on a nationwide tour. He landed in *The Spirit of St. Louis* and rode in an open-top car with the governor and the mayor through downtown. Facing page: the procession at Main Street and Broadway. From there, Lindbergh's caravan went to the fairgrounds and to Oklahoma City University, where he spoke briefly to an estimated 4,000 people about the country's need for airports.

# A new Capitol

Seven years after statehood and four years after state government moved to Oklahoma City from Guthrie, hundreds of Oklahomans gathered on a midsummer day at a tract of vacant land northeast of downtown. There, officials broke ground for a new Capitol building. The crowd, possibly egged on by the presence of movie cameras, proved difficult to restrain. After some delay, Governor Lee Cruce and leaders of the construction effort arrived in a small fleet of automobiles. According to an account of that day, July 20, 1914, Cruce stepped from his car and "with a mighty swing, drove a silver pick into the ground."

"I thank God it can no longer be charged that
Oklahoma, our state, is homeless."

— *Governor Lee Cruce*

The day's ceremonial speaking and digging was done entirely by
men, though one redoubtable woman tried to make it otherwise.
Anna Laskey, a suffragist who would serve in the state House of
Representatives in the 1920s and who in 1914 was a candidate
for commissioner of corrections and charities, asked to join the
ceremonies. Organizers rebuffed her, giving as a reason that
Oklahoma women did not have the right to vote.

Right, top and bottom: The cornerstone of Tishomingo granite
was laid November 16, 1915.

# Silver Screen

"Pride of the Southwest," publicists called Warner Brothers' Midwest Theater when it opened August 1, 1930, with a World War I drama, "Dawn Patrol." Facing page: People flocked to the ticket booth of the movie house, situated at ground level of the million-dollar, 10-story Midwest Building.

# All out for cooking advice!

One local celebrity consistently brought out crowds in the 1930s — Aunt Susan. Her regular newspaper column on cooking and her regular program on WKY radio delivered advice in a friendly, nearly folksy manner. Her readers and listeners filled the hall at Market Square Garden on October 12, 1930, right, to hear the first of a weeklong series of presentations on food preparation. Susan Abercrombie was *The Oklahoman*'s original Aunt Susan but, when Edna Vance took over the job in 1928, she kept the same pseudonym. Aunt Susan kept it up until 1943.

## Splashers

Preceding page: Summer vacation for kids started gloriously at Glen Ellyn Park in June 1935. These bathers frolicked for the photographer while adults and other children in streetclothes watched.

## The bounding main

Winds reached 32 miles per hour, creating choppy waters, damaging gear and occasionally capsizing boats at the city's first invitational sailboat regatta on June 18, 1939. But a few intrepid skippers and crew, who had brought their craft to Lake Overholser from Oklahoma, Kansas and Texas, made it to the finish line. The crew of this Snipe-class boat, left, rounded the mark and kept control of the sheets through the high winds, waves and spray.

## Solitude on ice

A week of subfreezing weather left a sheet of ice on Lake Overholser at the end of January 1936. That was enough for Nebraska-born Wallace Bohlke, a college student in nearby Bethany, to take a spin across the lake.

# Escaping the ordinary

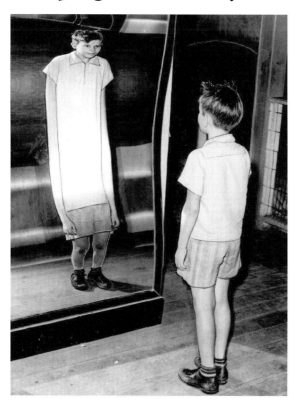

Springlake Amusement Park opened in the 1920s, the outgrowth of a spring-fed pond that its owner developed into a swimming and picnicking spot. In years to come, the park would add a pool, a roller coaster and other attractions — including funny mirrors, above. This one caught the attention of young Milton Johnson in 1939. Visitors paid no park entrance fee, instead purchasing entrance to individual rides such as the ferris wheel, right ...

... and bumper cars.

On a hot August day in 1939, the public fountains at Springlake Park proved refreshing.

Rising, falling and all the while spinning on the Tumble Bug at Springlake.

There were other attractions in Oklahoma City, too, among them this water slide at Shepherd's Lake. Dozens of children kept it busy in August 1930.

Public parks had their own rides, all of them free. These children hung on and spun around at Memorial Park.

A massive amphitheater was built by Civilian Conservation Corps workers at Lincoln Park and dedicated on Easter Sunday, April 12, 1936. An estimated 15,000 to 17,000 people turned out for a sunrise service.

Elsewhere at Lincoln Park, the young CCC workers, supervised by the National Park Service, also constructed a rustic marker at the park's Eastern Avenue entrance. In addition, they built a picnic ground, bathhouse and stone bridge.

# The big show

At the heart of Lincoln Park's attractions was the zoo, and the star of the zoo was Luna, the elephant. The animal was trained by Leo Blondin, since 1930 director of the zoo. Blondin's background was in the circus and in trained-animal acts. He led Luna through her paces, below, for appreciative audiences.

Luna let children pet her and ogle her, even in the parade welcoming her to Oklahoma City, above. Leo Blondin not only ran the zoo and trained animals, but also tended to the more prosaic work of trimming Luna's nails. He promoted the zoo regularly on his "Uncle Leo" radio program.

Facing page: A member of Blondin's staff washed down the elephant.

The zoo's collection ranged from exotic animals such as water buffalo, top, and camels, left, to commonplace North American species such as raccoons, above.

In the early 1930s, visitors also could see a baboon and a tiger.

# Champs

The Oklahoma City Order of the Rainbow girls' drill team, winner of a first prize at the annual state Rainbow convention in 1930 at Chickasha.

## The sporting scene

In the days before television, the highest level of baseball that fans could watch in Oklahoma City was played by the Indians, a minor-league team that dated from 1909. The Indians played in various leagues on various fields in the city with varying success. In 1929, they were managed by former major-leaguer Al "Lefty" Leifield, who went through a series of signs from the coaching box. Leifield led the team for only one season, finishing third in the Western League. The 1939 team, above, finished seventh of eight clubs in the Texas League.

Bob Hunt of Classen High School won the high jump at the 1934 state track meet with a mark of 5 feet, 11 inches. Trying to set a new Oklahoma record, however, Hunt failed to clear 6 feet, 1 ½ inches.

The city fielded a minor professional hockey team in the middle 1930s called the Warriors. They played on a rink inside the Stockyards Coliseum, but only briefly and without posting a winning record. In the midst of their third season, the Warriors moved to Minneapolis.

The Professional Golfers' Association brought its championship to Oklahoma City in October 1935. Paul Runyan tried to fight his way out of the sand trap, right, but lost his semifinal round at Twin Hills Golf & Country Club to Al Zimmerman. In the end, Johnny Revolta won the PGA title.

The city's first organized polo team came to life on a field in Nichols Hills. Each Sunday morning, the players scrimmaged. Right: Stables of the Oklahoma City Saddle and Riding Club.

This building in Nichols Hills would house the Oklahoma City Golf and Country Club, which in 1930 swapped its old property for the newly landscaped acreage.

# For the nimble of fingers

Only months into "Alfalfa Bill" Murray's term as governor, in May 1931, the first couple staged an all-state quilting bee at the Governor's Mansion for participants 75 years old and older. The quilters were chosen by state senators and by the governor and his wife.

For all the pleasure offered by parades, ceremonies, sports and other distractions, Oklahoma City in the 1930s also faced grim news on several fronts. Like the rest of the United States, Oklahoma was swept up in the Great Depression. Like other parts of the Great Plains, the city and the state year after year faced drought, dust and insufferable heat.

## THE DAILY OKLAHOMAN

The Weather

182,814

(AP) MEANS ASSOCIATED PRESS — FIFTY-TWO PAGES—OKLAHOMA CITY, SUNDAY, AUGUST 5, 1934.

SINGLE COPY PRICE Daily 5c; Sunday 10c

# WHOLE STATE PLACED IN DROUTH AREA

*Pilot Perfects Brake to Land Speedy Ships in Small Area*

**G. O. P. STIFLES FIGHT ON HEAD OF PARTY UNIT**

Hawk Says He Will Not Quit Post, Denies Any Row Is Likely.

**TO DRAW PLATFORM**

Proposals to Go Before Parley to Be Drafted By Group Today.

**800,000 On Relief Rolls In Mid-west**

**GILES TO ASK $3,000,000 OF FEDERAL FUND**

Survey Shows Oklahoma Has 100,635 Families On Aid Lists.

**SAYS SHARE IS LOW**

New Designation Will Extend Help to All Sections Soon.

**MOIST COLLAR DAYS TO STAY**

**PICKETS BRING COURT ACTION**

**Treasure Ship Divers Tell Of Battles With Devilfish**

Octopii Were Worst Of Horrors Found In Dark Green Waters Off Alaskan Coast

**DEATH CLAIMS DOCTOR'S WIFE**

Mrs. E. S. Ferguson, Active In Music, Social Work, Ill Only 10 Days.

*Scourge of Blistering Sun Shrivels Oklahoma Under Five-Day Blast of Heat*

**June Records Are Shattered When Mercury Again Leaves Century Mark Behind.**

**Rescued From Fire Flames Lick at Pallet**

**In 1299 We Had Real Drouth; Marks Still Show**

"A lot of good, rich Oklahoma soil" landed on Oklahoma City's Main Street on March 24, 1937, according to *The Daily Oklahoman*. Residents had seen it all before: the sky darkening with dust and sand. Just before this storm, fueled by dry areas farther west, the city received scattered showers.

In 1935, dust blew on several occasions in March and April, when high winds carried in dirt from the panhandles of Oklahoma and Texas, southeastern Colorado and southwestern Kansas. As spring turned to summer in the middle 1930s, record high temperatures were recorded.

Right: Lake Overholser, primary source of Oklahoma City's water, suffered continuing insults from the weather in the 1930s.

Ice covered Lake Overholser's spillways as 1935 began. Barely more than a year later, below right, pleasure boats sat in mud as water receded from piers. In early April 1938, 50-mph winds in the middle of a blizzard damaged the banks of the lake, below left. On most such occasions, the city water supply was imperiled.

Facing page: Sometimes, the water dropped so low that an automobile could navigate parts of the lake bottom.

By summer 1930, scores and then hundreds of unemployed lined up at the state-federal labor bureau on Dewey Avenue, hoping to find work. The superintendent told *The Daily Oklahoman* that he distributed the jobs according to need. Although jobs often were temporary and paid poorly, the idea was to keep the applicants from starving.

# Seeking work and relief...

Boxes, bottles and old rags: In September 1934, workers for the Federal Emergency Relief Administration scoured Oklahoma City for anything in the way of rummage. After repairs, the items would be used to furnish homes of those who got jobs through FERA, an early New Deal agency aimed at providing households some kind of employment.

The FERA established a cannery, right, to pack meat.  The government had bought and killed livestock because of the drought.

## ...and a place to live

Applicants for public assistance crowded into lines at the new federal relief headquarters on NW 7 Street, left, in March 1934.

Right top: Poor families who had camped in lowlands near the North Canadian River were evacuated when heavy rains caused the river to flood and threaten the camps. A temporary tent city was built in Northwest Park and, when the river receded, the occupants were moved back to their homes. Meanwhile, the city looked for a permanent location for them.

Right bottom: Groups calling themselves "Hunger Delegations" from depressed areas around the state sat in the galleries of the Oklahoma Senate and House of Representatives, hoping for more state aid.

Will Rogers Courts, a 37-acre housing project for low-income residents, was built by the Public Works Administration in 1936 and 1937 near the meatpacking district. The project aimed to provide not only housing but also work for the construction industry.

Facing page: By October 1937, families at Will Rogers Courts were inspecting their new quarters.

Oil wells had sprouted across Oklahoma for years but, until the late 1920s, no oil had been discovered in Oklahoma City itself. On December 4, 1928, Henry V. Foster's Indian Territory Illuminating Oil Company brought in this well, touching off a boom that would see derricks rise across the city. The new oil wealth did not reach everyone, but it took some of the sting out of the Great Depression.

# Wild Mary

Striking oil sometimes had its downside. On the morning of March 26, 1930, workers were pulling tools out of the hole at the No. 1 Mary Sudik well so that a new bit could be installed. The crew failed to fill the hole with mud during the process, and when only a few joints remained to be pulled out, natural gas broke through with a roar. Pipe was blasted to the top of the rig. It fell and warped the legs of the derrick. As hours went by, the gas turned to a gusher of oil that coated pasture, farm houses and cattle. The fountain of oil went on for 11 days, and newspapers and radio stations across the country recounted the story of "Wild Mary." After the well finally was capped, left, local officials passed ordinances to increase safety procedures and to regulate spacing of wells.

Drilling spread even to the grounds of the Capitol.

Facing page: By the end of the 1930s derricks were lined up like sentries.

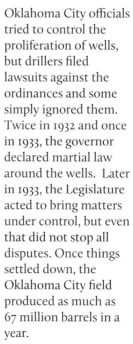

Oklahoma City officials tried to control the proliferation of wells, but drillers filed lawsuits against the ordinances and some simply ignored them. Twice in 1932 and once in 1933, the governor declared martial law around the wells. Later in 1933, the Legislature acted to bring matters under control, but even that did not stop all disputes. Once things settled down, the Oklahoma City field produced as much as 67 million barrels in a year.

This well on the statehouse grounds collapsed over the noon hour in August 1937, when a part of the derrick gave way, putting uneven weight on the rest of the structure.

Facing page: During the oil boom of the 1930s, derricks stood next to homes and schools — and even hospitals.

In a lightning storm on July 20, 1936, a well on NE 17 Street spouted oil from a 40-foot vent pipe over three city blocks. Coming through open windows of homes, the oil spattered furniture, walls and fixtures. Outside, it coated automobiles, lawns and trees. Mrs. G. K. Sutton, top right, was pouring lemonade for her husband and two guests when the oil struck. Only days before, a well two blocks away had burst into flames.

Months later, in September, another well nearby sprayed homes in a two-block area, top left. Workers trying to stop the flow were slathered in petroleum.

School was out for the summer, and the playground of Webster Junior High School became the staging ground for another well, right.

In the early 1930s, criminals had found irresistible the idea of kidnapping wealthy individuals or their relatives in return for ransom — even after the federal government made the crime punishable by death.

Sitting atop a fortune that made them one of the wealthiest couples in Oklahoma City, oilman Charles F. Urschel, upper right, and his wife, Berenice Urschel, right, served as prospective targets. Nevertheless, they adopted few if any security measures.

On the night of July 22, 1933, the Urschels were playing bridge on their screened porch with another oilman, Walter Jarrett, and his wife. About 11:15, two men, one with a machine gun and the other with a pistol, entered through the unlatched screen door and asked which of the men was Urschel. Receiving no answer, they marched both Urschel and Jarrett to the car they had parked near the Urschel garage, right, and drove away.

Eventually figuring out which captive was which, the kidnappers robbed Jarrett and quickly set him free. Not long afterward, Jarrett showed a newspaper photographer where Urschel was sitting the night of the crime, above. Four days after the event, a Tulsa oilman who was a friend of Urschel received a ransom demand for $200,000. On July 30, the ransom was delivered, as instructed by the kidnappers, in Kansas City. Urschel was freed the next day after nine days in captivity.

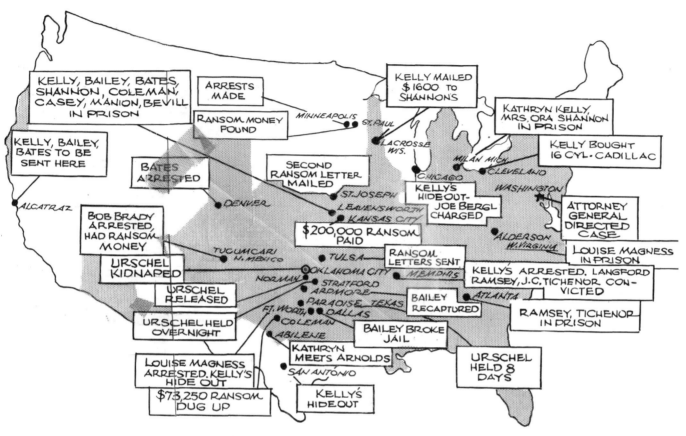

KELLY, BAILEY, BATES, SHANNON, COLEMAN, CASEY, MANION, BEVILL IN PRISON

ARRESTS MADE

KELLY MAILED $1600 TO SHANNONS

KATHRYN KELLY, MRS. ORA SHANNON IN PRISON

KELLY, BAILEY, BATES TO BE SENT HERE

RANSOM MONEY FOUND

MINNEAPOLIS

ST. PAUL

KELLY BOUGHT 16 CYL. CADILLAC

LACROSSE WIS.

BATES ARRESTED

SECOND RANSOM LETTER MAILED

MILAN MICH.

CLEVELAND

CHICAGO

KELLY'S HIDE OUT — JOE BERGL CHARGED

WASHINGTON

ATTORNEY GENERAL DIRECTED CASE

ALCATRAZ

DENVER

ST. JOSEPH

LEAVENWORTH

KANSAS CITY

BOB BRADY ARRESTED, HAD RANSOM MONEY

$200,000 RANSOM PAID

ALDERSON W. VIRGINIA

LOUISE MAGNESS IN PRISON

URSCHEL KIDNAPED

TUCUMCARI N. MEXICO

TULSA

RANSOM LETTERS SENT

KELLY'S ARRESTED. LANGFORD RAMSEY, J.C. TICHENOR CONVICTED

URSCHEL RELEASED

OKLAHOMA CITY

NORMAN

MEMPHIS

STRATFORD

ARDMORE

PARADISE, TEXAS

BAILEY RECAPTURED

ATLANTA

RAMSEY, TICHENOR IN PRISON

URSCHEL HELD OVERNIGHT

FT. WORTH

DALLAS

COLEMAN

BAILEY BROKE JAIL

LOUISE MAGNESS ARRESTED. KELLY'S HIDE OUT

ABILENE

KATHRYN MEETS ARNOLDS

URSCHEL HELD 8 DAYS

$73,250 RANSOM DUG UP

SAN ANTONIO

KELLY'S HIDE OUT

Although blindfolded much of the time, Urschel memorized details of his kidnapping that led authorities to Paradise, Texas, where Urschel had been held in two buildings, bottom left. Before long, the two suspected kidnappers were identified as George "Machine Gun" Kelly, right in bottom center photograph, and Albert Bates, above. Both were hunted down, Kelly famously in Memphis where he was said to have shouted, "Don't shoot, G-men!", thus giving FBI agents a nickname that stuck. Bates was caught in Denver. Within weeks, agents arrested Harvey Bailey, who was thought to have led the kidnapping, and a dozen other people connected to the crime, which had nationwide tentacles, above left. In the end, 20 people were convicted in connection with the crime. Baily, Kelly and Kelly's wife were sentenced to life in prison.

Two big banks merged in January 1930, and these Oklahoma City police armed themselves against the possibility that $20 million in cash, securities and other assets might tempt robbers. The riches were transferred a distance of two blocks after the merger of the American-First National Bank with Security National Bank. The resulting institution was named First National Bank and Trust Company.

The force showed off a van used to transport prisoners, above, and lined up its World War veterans for a group portrait, weapons and all, left.

Worried about an uptick in crime, the police in 1931 established a firing range near the North Canadian River and required detectives and officers to practice.

# Prohibition

"Dry" forces enshrined prohibition of alcoholic beverages in the constitution when Oklahoma became a state, and things stayed that way even as nationwide Prohibition came and went. After the end of national Prohibition in 1933, despite the arguments of Dry leaders, right, beer was legalized as a way to obtain revenue for the state. But the ban against hard liquor remained. Oklahoma County sheriff's deputies, below, cracked open barrels of liquor taken in raids in April 1935 and flushed the liquid down the sewer.

One sure way authorities could gather a crowd was to dump illegal alcohol into the streets. Wags among the smiling onlookers reached down as the booze flowed past.

## Vice

Liquor wasn't the only product confiscated by police. In summer 1935, sheriff's deputies and jail trusties smashed slot machines that had been taken in gambling raids, left. Early the next year, above, the police began looking into the sale of lewd magazines by drugstores and newsstands near city schools.

The 1920s saw two Oklahoma governors in a row elected, impeached and removed from office.

## Jack Walton

The first to go was Jack Walton, the fifth governor since statehood. He was elected in 1922, above, as a progressive Democrat and took office in January 1923. In his first months, he led the way to enactment of new laws to aid troubled farms, provide free textbooks to all Oklahoma students and increase spending for education and welfare. But before his first year was out, Walton began to waver in his progressive views and lost much of his support. Hoping to quell the Ku Klux Klan and racial unrest, he declared martial law in two counties, and later imposed martial law on the entire state, above right. By November 1923, angry legislators — a substantial number of whom held Klan membership — impeached Walton and removed him from office, below right.

## A new governor's mansion

Oklahoma acquired land for a governor's mansion in 1914 but, until the oil boom brought money flowing into the state's coffers, nothing happened to the property. In 1927, in the first year of Governor Henry Johnston's term, legislators appropriated $100,000 for the house and furnishings. After plans were trimmed down to match the appropriation, the mansion was built. In 1928, the governor and his family moved in.

# Henry Johnston

After the ousted Governor Walton's lieutenant governor completed the last three years of his term, Oklahomans elected Henry Johnston to the state's highest office. Like Walton, Johnston fell from favor with legislators. After two years in office, he, too, was impeached after a nasty battle in which Johnston called out the National Guard to enforce martial law to keep the Legislature from meeting to impeach him.

His term began well enough. The crowd at Johnston's inauguration in January 1927 was estimated at 20,000, and he and his wife led a grand procession at the inaugural ball, left. Things started well with the Legislature, which approved his plans to increase state aid to schools and build a hospital for crippled children. But soon complaints arose about his private secretary, who was said to be making decisions for the governor. Before Johnston's first year was out, the Legislature met in special session to try to impeach him. The state Supreme Court ruled the Leglslature out of order and Johnston ordered the National Guard to keep legislators out of the Capitol. In the midst of it all, the Johnstons posed for a 1928 Christmas picture, below left.

The Legislature, under the state constitution, did not meet again until 1929. That January, it succeeded in impeaching Johnston and quickly suspended him from office. By the end of March, it had removed him entirely on a charge of general incompetence. His wife, Ethel Johnston, watched from her car as workers removed the family furnishings from the governor's mansion. The Johnstons had been the first family to occupy it.

# Alfalfa Bill

Having seen both his elected predecessors removed from office, William Murray — a flamboyant lawyer who helped craft the state constitution in the early 1900s — ran for and won the governorship in 1930.

Murray was a fiery orator who earlier in his career urged farmers to diversify with crops such as alfalfa. That earned him the nickname, "Alfalfa Bill." Inaugurated in 1931, right, top and bottom, he entered what would prove to be a colorful four-year term.

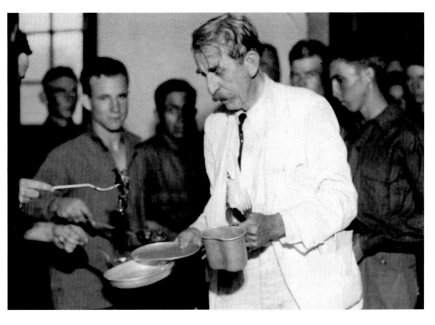

U.S. HIGHWAY 75
"This Highway to Texas & the Red River Bridge opened to the free use of the public by Governor William H. Murray of Okla. July 16.1931. This Highway on the Texas side closed by Governor Ross S. Sterling of Texas with Texas Rangers July 17.1931."

Often Murray called out the National Guard to enforce his policies. Perhaps the most notable incident came when a dispute arose between him and the owners of toll bridges over the Red River to Texas. The state built a free bridge and Murray went there to personally take charge of the Guard, below. He exchanged salutes, above left, and ate with the troops.

Murray despised President Franklin Roosevelt and the New Deal. When federal agencies tried to distribute relief to poor Oklahomans, Murray hindered the effort. Five months after his term ended, Murray gave an interview to *The Daily Oklahoman*, blasting the New Deal and threatening to switch to the Republican Party "if necessary, to save the Constitution." He continued, "Relief — the dole — has broken the morale of our people." He also made increasingly racist and anti-Semitic comments. Murray ran for governor again in 1938, but lost the Democratic primary.

Facing page: the Governor's Mansion from the air in early 1936, after Murray had been succeeded by Ernest Marland

Following pages: The inauguration crowd for Marland, in January 1935. Unlike the governors of the 1920s, Marland was not impeached and removed. Unlike Murray, he welcomed New Deal programs to Oklahoma. Like his predecessors, he had a contentious relationship with the Legislature and accomplished relatively little in his term.

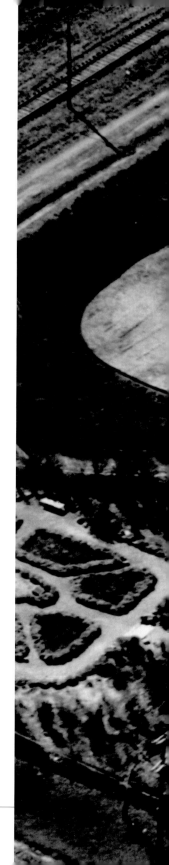

The economic hardship of the Great Depression and New Deal protections for labor unions brought on increases in union membership and union activity in Oklahoma.

Coal miners, smelting workers, textile workers and refinery workers all struck from time to time, as did workers in the packing industry. In early June 1934, meatpackers walked out of the Wilson and Armour plants and the Oklahoma National Stockyards, seeking higher wages and a minimum number of weekly hours of work. These workers met cars at the gate to Packingtown, above and facing page, top, in an attempt to halt strikebreakers. Police were ordered to the scene to try to keep things peaceful.

After 10 days, the strikers returned to work, and both sides claimed a small victory as union workers re-entered the plant, bottom.

One year after the 1934 strike, four hundred union workers at the Wilson plant walked out. The company brought in non-union workers and promptly claimed the plant was fully operational. Women, top right, held signs at a street corner outside the plant backing the union cause. Later that month, picketers showed up outside groceries that sold Wilson Products, such as Edwards Brothers on North Blackwelder Avenue, bottom right, urging customers not to buy. The pickets stayed only a few hours and then were removed by the union. The 1935 meatpackers strike lasted seven months until a settlement was reached.

## The Civic Center

In 1927, Oklahoma City voters approved a bond issue to remove the Rock Island railroad tracks in the heart of downtown and to make way for new local government buildings on the site. The tracks were gone within a couple of years; the new buildings took a while to replace them. Drawn-out disputes over sites for the buildings and lawsuits over properties continued through the early 1930s. The Depression also slowed matters, but new buildings began to rise with the help of federal money.

Preceding page: By 1936, riveters were at work on the Civic Center's steel structure.

Right: Steelworker Bill Weatherford posed happily in the midst of work on the Civic Center.

Facing page: In April 1937, the complex was taking shape. At right stood the Oklahoma County Courthouse. City Hall lay just beyond it and the Municipal Auditorium and police building beyond that.

Inside, the new Civic Center buildings showed the art deco influence popular in the era's architecture. Above, a stairway at City Hall. Top right and right, a longhorn motif and massive chandelier at the Courthouse. Far right, the mirrored entrance inside the Municipal Auditorium.

In late November 1936, while the Civic Center buildings were still under construction, workers built a non-working derrick with a shiny frame as Oklahoma City prepared to host the Independent Petroleum Association of America.

In March 1937, the time came to move to the new offices in the Civic Center. Two City Hall employees, J.L. Beveridge, left, and Mike Peshek, joked for a photographer about how they would share the burden of moving to the new space.

He grew up the son of a successful Oklahoma rancher, but Will Rogers relished the world beyond the ranch. Hopping steamers, he made his way as a young man across the Atlantic and worked in the entertainment business, doing rope tricks in Wild West shows and circuses. The tricks and his humorous comments led to the New York stage and then to Hollywood. From there, he branched out to book-writing, radio broadcasting and speaking engagements. Newspapers across the country carried his syndicated column about issues of the day, right. Among them was *The Daily Oklahoman*.

## Oklahoman | Sunday, August 24, 1930 | 16

*We never could find out what the governor would give.*

## Once World Owed Us Living, Now Its Auto, Radio and Clara Bow, He Opines.

### By WILL ROGERS

WELL, all I know is just what I read in the papers. Now I have been perusing the Periodicals with an eagle eye, and to save my soul I cant see a thing that will bear repeating. Premature Golf has got us by the ears, and America has a putter in its hand. Its been a godsend to vacant lots. They look beautiful at nights, but in the day time when the lights are not on, the Gingerbread kinder crops out. But its been a great thing, the working men who put them in, and at a time when Prosperity was at what you might say was its lowest ebb. In fact it wasent even ebbing.

They say "It started in old Chatanooga a long time ago." Now I know Chatanooga pretty well, its a great old town. Lookout Mountain is perched at its doorstep. Adol— lisher and Owner o— York Times comes — this Snare Drum C— from there has got — publicity than Mr. Oc— of Chicamauga, or Lo— or even the Bend in th— at it you wouldent th— the City that was t— whole of America "pi— putting it dowh" —

BUT those ola s— mighty ingenious. It was a Guy in Memph— this Piggly Wiggly busin— that if somebody give yo— told you to go to it, t— take up more junk than— was digging it out fo— woman instinct would n— her believe that the fell— the bag at the finish m— something.

But anyhow he made — of it, and say, by the wa— ask him, that man Saun— of his own name) what — with that invention for p— mobiles. He took me wh— Memphis one time and s— working model of it, and — the time that it was the greatest thing I had ever seen. It was a gig like an elevator, with cages on both sides. One coming down—

Cal. or old Rogers County, Okla., or Brown County, Indiana.

We are just stepping too fast. In the old days we figured the world owed us a living, now we figure he owes us an Automobile, a Player Piano, and Radio, Frigid Air, and Clara Bow. The Automobile is to take you places you would be better off if you dident go to. The player Piano is to discourage you from trying to play your own simple little tunes that your folks spent so much on your learning. The Radio is for President. The Frigid air is too give you ice water when you would be better off if you dident load upon it, and Clara Bow will just lead you plum astray. She will give a Country boy the wrong —

### Horse and Buggy Days Not So Dumb When It Came To Nifty Whoopee, Says Will

IF I'M ELECTED
I WILL GIVE
RIDE 'IM COW BOY!
HOOK HIM COW!
WATCH THAT BULL BUCK!
WHAT A BULL!
RIDE 'IM PRETTY
ATA BOY!

In 1913, a teenaged Wiley Post saw his first airplane in flight at a county fair in Lawton. That hooked him on aviation, but it was not until the early 1920s — while working in the Oklahoma oil fields — that he learned how to fly. Despite losing one eye in an oil-rig accident, Post went on to become personal pilot to Oklahoma oilman F.C. Hall, who bought a Lockheed Vega airplane that Hall named the *Winnie Mae*, after his daughter. By 1930, Post was winning airplane races, and the next year, with navigator Harold Gatty, he flew the *Winnie Mae* on a northern route around the world in less than nine days. In the process, Post gained world fame. In 1931, Post hobnobbed with fellow Oklahoma celebrity Will Rogers, above, in Claremore, Oklahoma.

In July 1931, Oklahoma City honored Wiley Post with a parade through downtown. Riding with him was his navigator, Harold Gatty, above, right, and his chief backer and employer, oilman F.C. Hall, who waved to the crowd.

Later, Post flew around the world alone and also experimented with high-altitude flights, wearing a pressure suit of his own design. In 1935, he continued to experiment by placing floats on a Lockheed Orion to see how it would survive long flight. Will Rogers, who needed new material for his column, joined Post on a flight that was scheduled to take them to Alaska and then Siberia. Taking off from a lagoon near Point Barrow, Alaska, the aircraft crashed. Post and Rogers both died in the accident. After the bodies of Post and Rogers were returned to the Lower 48, services for Rogers were conducted in California and in Claremore, Oklahoma. Post's body was brought to Oklahoma City, where a military escort carried it to the Capitol.

The body lay in state at the Capitol, above right, where thousands of people bade Wiley Post farewell. After Governor Ernest Marland addressed the mourners on the Capitol steps, above, Post's funeral was held at Oklahoma City's First Baptist Church, where his widow, Mae Laine, was escorted in.

Post's name went on an Oklahoma City airport. Rogers' went on a highway that stretched from Chicago to southern California, Route 66.

## Aviation

Technology's progress in 20th-century Oklahoma City registered not only in the feats of Wiley Post, but also among lesser known folks such as Alberta Worley, left, the city's first licensed female pilot. In 1929, she staged aerial shows at Municipal Airport. Also a full participant in the Aviation Age was Rex Rowland, right, who managed the hangar at the airport and who in 1933 earned his own pilot's license.

Above: The hangar at Curtiss-Wright field, built by the airplane company northwest of the city in 1928. The field was renamed Wiley Post Airport in 1941, after the aviator who used it from 1929 to 1934 to experiment with airplanes. From 1932 to 1937, the field also was the home of Braniff Airways.

## Home Town Forum Toasts Braniff

### Air Commerce Figures Join in Praise.

THE lone, old-fashioned plane from which grew one of the country's leading airlines was lauded and an Oklahoma City citizen was praised by some of aviation's greats Friday at the Oklahoma City Chamber of Commerce.

The program was held to honor T. E. Braniff, president of the Braniff Airways Co., for the tenth anniversary of his company.

Those who have seen the single plane expand into a service that covers territory from the Great Lakes to the Gulf, gathered with the dignitaries of the air to pay homage to th man who has done most to bring about that progress.

While praises were crowded on his shoulders, Braniff, his wife, and son, sat in embarrassed silence. Braniff, however, made the principal address, minimizing the importance of his line's expansion and the credit due to himself.

Walter Dean, who was mayor when Braniff Airways were born, retold the story of the line's early existence. E. M. Fry, former city manager, recalled the date, September of 1930, when the Municipal airport property was acquired, thereby "putting Oklahoma City on the air map of the United States."

*T. E. Braniff*

THESE former city officials no longer are in city offices, but the present administration was there, to state that it, too, believes that Braniff is an important part of the city's life.

"We are proud to have a fellow citizen who has so developed a rapidly developing industry," said Mayor Frank Martin, W. A. Quinn, city manager, added his praises.

Not all of the praise came from fellow citizens. Col. Edgar S. Gorrell, Chicago, president of the Air Transport Association of America, spoke of

### "10-Year Growth Of Air Line Told.

the "enviable safety record" of the Braniff company. To show the progress of aviation since the birth of the Braniff line, Colonel Gorrell said that "over 1,000 more passengers are in the air every second of the hour today."

"Such men as Tom Braniff and his associates have made all this possible," he said.

Wayne Parrish, Washington, editor of American Aviation, spoke of the "important part" Braniff has played in development of aviation.

OTHER visitors included Major E. M. Haight, New Orleans, regional supervisor of the bureau of air commerce; T. E. Flaherty, Little Rock, Ark., district advisor, bureau of air commerce; Hal Henning, Dallas, aircraft distributor; Joe Shumate, Dallas, division inspector, bureau of air commerce; George Hoddaway, Fort Worth, editor of Southern Flight magazine; W. G. Skelly, Tulsa; and delegations from Corpus Christi, Texas; Wichita, Kan.; Brownsville, Texas; Waco, Texas; Wichita Falls, Texas; Fort Worth, Texas, and Kansas City, Mo.

John Kroutil, Yukon; J. M. Gentry, commissioner of public safety; C. R. Mooney, Kansas City, secretary of the Southwest Aviation conference, and others were introduced.

Oklahoma City had a firm place in commercial aviation as the one-time home of Thomas E. Braniff, an Oklahoma City insurance executive who, with his brother, Paul, founded Braniff Airways. Until World War II, the airline would be based in Oklahoma City. Later it moved to Dallas. In summer 1938, above, Thomas Braniff was honored by the Oklahoma City Chamber of Commerce.

# Broadcasting

Begun as an experimental station by a World War I veteran in the early 1920s, WKY was purchased in 1928 by Edward K. Gaylord, who also was publisher of *The Daily Oklahoman*. The station produced many of its own shows, among them the Harmony Boys on Thursday nights in 1929, above. Sunday mornings at 8, Eugene Maple read *The Oklahoman*'s comics over the air — purportedly to relieve parents of the chore. In 1936, the station opened studios in the Skirvin Tower, where it boasted a fully equipped sound-effects room, top.

The curious jammed Municipal Auditorium on November 14, 1939, to see the miracle of television. Behind banks of intense lights and microphones, the Rough Riders, a WKY radio musical group, performed as part of a demonstration of the new technology. Viewing screens were set up at the back of the room.

Even with advances in petroleum production, aviation, broadcasting and other wonders of the 20th century, just outside Oklahoma City lay farmland that remained productive. At the 27-acre Andy Shaver farm east of Eastern Avenue, left, the 1938 wheat harvest — done with mule power — was under way in early June. Across the plains that year, the crop was expected to be bountiful — and per-bushel prices were expected to be low.

A lifelong Oklahoma County farmer, 25-year-old Ralph White, and his 21-year-old wife, Zenobia White, right, received the chance to live out an experiment arranged by the Oklahoma City Chamber of Commerce. They were to test the effects of long-term tenancy — in the Whites' case five years — against year-to-year leasing. Their tenancy was to be on 80 acres owned by Oklahoma Gas & Electric Company. Ralph White agreed to clear brush, fix fences and maintain the farm in good condition. Also, he was to plant 10 acres of legumes and treat the land with phosphate or lime annually. The rest the couple could do with as they wished. Their new home represented an upgrade in their living standard.

At the Oklahoma City National Stockyards, judges trooped along a line of cattle shown by 4-H Club members and Future Farmers of America at their livestock show in March 1934.

The stockyards dated to 1910 and the meatpackers who built plants there also created a livestock exchange. Later, local entrepreneurs added a coliseum for stock shows and rodeos. The first coliseum, built in 1922, had folding wooden chairs in the balcony and box seats along with temporary seating on the floor, top right. When that building burned in 1930, it was quickly rebuilt, bottom right.

The Oklahoma City National Stockyards in the middle 1930s. Livestock marketing was the city's first major industry.

Herbert Jones, agriculture instructor at Capitol Hill  Senior High School in the background, was busy cutting wheat and oats in 1935.

*The Farmer-Stockman* began life as a weekly version of *The Daily Oklahoman*. In 1911, it was renamed, converted to magazine format and refocused entirely on agriculture. In the 1930s, *The Farmer-Stockman* promoted annual tours. The 1937 destination was Alaska and the Yukon, and it was announced that local cooking expert Aunt Susan would go along on the trip. A few of that year's 117 participants waved from the rear platform of their train on departure day from Oklahoma City.

Streetcars began running in Oklahoma City in 1903 and, until the advent of affordable automobiles in the 1920s, they helped shape the city. Twentieth-century streetcar travel began as a private venture by Anton Classen and John Shartel, who opened an electric-powered system that served downtown.

The system eventually grew to 168 miles of track. In early January 1940, the system brought its snowplows out of storage to clear the tracks after a storm dumped nearly six inches on the city.

The streetcar system radiated from the main terminal, above, but by 1940 the terminal was becoming less busy. Late that year, the system rid itself of outdated cars such as Old No. 84, left, which was draped in black for its final run. Also, the system abandoned some routes.

Battling declining ridership, railroads in the 1930s loved to show off their new products. On December 8, 1939, a Santa Fe streamliner made its debut at the Santa Fe station, left. The streamliner, pulled by a diesel locomotive, boasted cars with double-sealed windows and other modern touches. The schedule called for it to leave Oklahoma City at 6:45 a.m. each day, arrive in Kansas City by 1:45 and finish in Chicago by 9:30, cutting two hours off the existing Santa Fe time to Chicago. The occasion brought speeches by local officials, a christening ceremony, a radio broadcast and music by a kiltie band.

Right: Since the land run of 1889, Santa Fe trains had traveled on the surface, north and south through the center of the city. In the late 1920s, plans were made to elevate the line to reduce traffic jams caused by long trains. That work was completed in 1933. In 1934, a new Santa Fe station was built.

The Rock Island Railroad also ran on the surface, east and west through downtown, paralleled by the tracks of the Frisco. By 1930, throngs of automobiles were forced to wait for long trains to pass. That year, the city bought out the railroad property, and the tracks were rerouted south of downtown. Plans were made to build the Civic Center where the tracks once ran. Clockwise from upper left: site of the old Rock Island loading platform north of the Skirvin Hotel; fixing up new crossings; removing old track.

On November 30, 1930, with the mayor at the throttle and veteran developer Charles F. Colcord acting as fireman, the last Rock Island passenger train through the heart of downtown pulled out of the old station. A few blocks away, the honorary party stepped off the train to break ground for the Civic Center that would rise on the old railroad right-of-way. Then, one last freight chugged through downtown, blocking traffic for one final time.

The day after the ceremonies ending Rock Island traffic through downtown, the Rock Island and Frisco opened a temporary station. A passenger car was converted into a waiting room, complete with wooden benches and a newsstand. Meanwhile, the old station buildings were demolished.

The Rock Island *Rocket*, left, was introduced
to Oklahoma City in November 1938. The
streamliner made daily trips from Dallas through
Oklahoma City to Kansas City and back. The
engine room of the *Rocket* locomotive, above.

Facing page: In 1939, the Frisco dressed up some of its fast passenger locomotives and cut hours off the running time from Oklahoma City to Kansas City.

Frisco's sleek *Firefly*, above, was the first streamlined steam locomotive through the city on March 29, 1940. The engine looked modern, having been refurbished in Frisco's shops in Springfield, Missouri. However, the locomotive inside the sleek body was built in 1910. The *Firefly* was scheduled to travel about 70 mph on the trip from Oklahoma City through Tulsa to Kansas City.

The *Meteor*, left, was Frisco's Oklahoma City-St. Louis train. It ran overnight.

In November 1916, the six-story Capitol was taking shape near NE 23 Street and North Lincoln Boulevard. Bedford limestone covered most of the structure and work continued on the wings. Although the building was designed to allow for a dome to be added eventually, cost considerations weighed in the decision to eliminate it. The Capitol remained without a dome for decades. Construction finished on June 30, 1917.

The south front of the Capitol on a snowy night in late December 1935.

A mid-December snowfall in 1932 covered the Capitol and grounds, including the Oklahoma Historical Society Building.

Almost two decades after the Capitol was built, the view from the north front formed a monument to Oklahoma's oil economy — a row of gasoline stations, along with the headquarters of the Truck Owners Association just behind the gasoline station on the left.

A long wait for a license

The deadline for Oklahomans to get their 1939 driver's licenses was March 15 of that year and, as the days wound down, it turned out that many put things off until the last minute. On March 13, the line waiting to get to the tag agency at right stretched around the northwest corner of N 10 and Broadway. The state opened three additional offices over the final few days to try to alleviate the backup.

# The adoptables

The Holmes Home of Redeeming Love was established in 1900 in Guthrie by Free Methodist women who aimed to care for unwed mothers. It moved to farmland north of Oklahoma City in 1909, and established a nursing school in 1923. The home continually showed off its babies, and *The Daily Oklahoman* frequently published photos of groups of babies or single children, above and facing page, all of whom were available for adoption.

Left: The Sunbeam Home was begun in 1907 by a group of women who raised money to provide safe housing for homeless children. In 1929, children played baseball on the lawn of the home on W 21 Street.

Adopted once from the Home of Redeeming Love and returned, 20-month-old Lily, above, was deaf from birth. Obtaining a home for her, according to the nurses, proved difficult. *The Daily Oklahoman* headlined the item, "Lonely Life Looms for Orphaned Baby."

## At last, the bonus

For more than a decade, veterans of World War I had rankled at not receiving extra money for their service. In early 1936, Congress enacted a bonus plan for veterans that would issue bonds with 3 percent interest, which was better than prevailing savings rates. Veterans could hold them as investments until 1945 or redeem them for cash any time after June 15, 1936. In Oklahoma City, bonds were delivered June 16. At the post office, veterans jammed the registry window to get their bonds, which arrived by registered mail.

The next day, veterans by the hundreds lined up to cash in their just-received bonds. By 8 a.m. June 17, the line at Central High School extended down the steps and along the sidewalk. By 10 a.m., 600 veterans were waiting there.

## At the parades

In the 1930s, sundry occasions demanded a parade. In 1935, for the 25th anniversary of the opening of the stockyards, a Livestock Silver Jubilee Parade of Progress wound through downtown. This football-themed float featured members of Kappa Tau Delta sorority at Oklahoma City University.

The Petroleum Pageant of Progress Parade in late November 1936.

# Waiting out the show

When Aunt Susan staged her well-attended annual cooking school in the Oklahoma City Coliseum, participants could drop off their children at a supervised playroom. These kids behaved themselves for the photographer in October 1935, the fifth year of the weeklong presentations by Aunt Susan, the columnist and local radio chef whose real name was Edna Vance.

# New greenery

Washington's Birthday in 1937 marked the occasion for Girl Scouts to plant seven trees at Will Rogers Park. The park, formerly Northwest Park, was named for the late Oklahoma humorist in 1936.

# Public health

Stoically accepting his fate, Victor Lynn, a student at Putnam Heights School, underwent vaccination in November 1929. The city physician, W.H. Miles, administered the measure in public schools across Oklahoma City. Dr. Miles' bantering manner was said to have a calming effect on his patients.

## The ancient faith

Receiving an education in Judaism were these boys at Emanuel Synagogue in 1930. The synagogue, chartered in 1904 with 22 members, represented the Orthodox branch, which comprised many Jews who had immigrated from Eastern Europe around the turn of the century.

# Singing for the love of it

The Oklahoma City Mothers Chorus, 65 strong, rehearsed at Roosevelt Junior High School every Friday in late 1936 before doing Christmastime performances for the Council of Parents and Teachers and a Chamber of Commerce luncheon. The chorus would sing — upon invitation — before civic or social clubs and school groups.

## Willing to wait

At poll-closing time the evening of election day 1936, when President Franklin D. Roosevelt was up for re-election against Alf Landon, about 200 voters remained outside this precinct on NW 29. Election laws required officials to let them vote if they were on hand at the 7:30 closing, so the precinct stayed open until all had cast ballots.

# Reminders

The second World War was underway in Europe in November 1939 when Oklahoma City's YWCA chose the Armistice Day anniversary to show off a collection of World War I posters owned by Mrs. Walter S. Hanson. She had volunteered with the Red Cross and helped distribute the posters in the first war. The posters — which encouraged viewers to "make the world safe for democracy" and also evoked hatred for the enemy — were considered to have been among the most effective items in the World War I propaganda campaign waged by the United States. Mrs. Hanson said she hoped the posters would "remind a lot of us of the horror and anguish of war — and guide our thinking today."

## At the library

Depression-era habitues of the Carnegie Library made the newspaper room the most popular department in the building. According to the room's custodian, many of the avid readers stayed there, browsing through out-of-town newspapers, from opening time until closing.

# The question of race

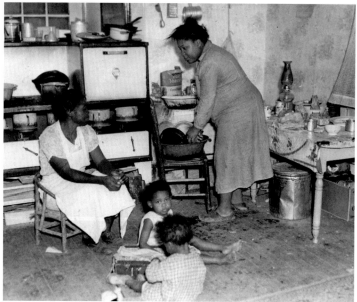

In late 1939, *The Daily Oklahoman* took on a subject that many, if not most, metropolitan newspapers of the time would not touch – the problem of housing in the black community. Under a headline, "Whose Responsibility?" the newspaper documented the sometimes miserable conditions under which black residents lived, above and right. "Scores of families," it said, "are cramped in ramshackle quarters without modern conveniences of any kind."

Above: Oklahoma City hosted the National Forensic League Tournament in May 1936, and Classen High School was filled with the declamations of about 500 teenage orators. One of the contestants was Caleb Peterson of Peekskill, New York, above, who at first was barred from Classen. Some tournament organizers had feared "contestants from the south" might object to competing with a black orator and planned to have Peterson and three judges move to an all-black high school for his three speeches. The executive council decided otherwise, and Peterson spoke at the same high school as everyone else.

# Visitors from the White House

First lady Eleanor Roosevelt visited Oklahoma City in early March 1937, speaking twice at the Shrine auditorium, and meeting with reporters and others, including women of the Women's Jeffersonian League. In late October 1939, she returned at the invitation of the Altrusa Club, above. She also met with Girl Scouts and Camp Fire Girls and with the press.

President Franklin D. Roosevelt came through town on July 9, 1938. He was cheered by crowds along the streets as his motorcade took him to a speech at Fair Park. Oklahoma City was one of the stops on Roosevelt's cross-country tour in support of candidates for Congress, specifically Senator Elmer Thomas of Oklahoma, right. Oklahoma City Mayor J. Frank Martin, at the lectern, introduced the president. Between Martin and Roosevelt stood a bodyguard.

# The law: Making and deciding it

The speaker of the Oklahoma House of Representatives called to order a new legislative session on January 6, 1931, before a packed gallery, facing page. Even on opening day, some members were propping their feet on desks.

Only 33 years of age, Alfred P. Murrah, right, was sworn in on March 12, 1937, as the youngest federal judge in the United States. His fellow U.S. district judges doing the honors were Edgar S. Vaught, left, of Oklahoma City and Robert L. Williams of Muskogee. As a youth, Murrah had ridden freight cars, washed dishes and sold newspapers. He made his way through the University of Oklahoma and, after joining the bar, Murrah specialized in workers compensation and personal injury cases. At the recommendation of one of his professors, whom Murrah had helped along in politics, he was named to the federal court. In 1940, Murrah rose to the U.S. 10th Circuit Court of Appeals.

## Educators all

More than 7,000 members of the Oklahoma Education Association jammed the Stockyards Coliseum for the first general session of their annual state convention on February 6, 1936. Speakers urged the teachers to demand more federal and state aid for schools — and to guard against assaults on existing state support. "The schools must compete with all the agencies of state government for funds," association President L.E. Wheeler told the crowd.

## Just looking

Weekend window shoppers strolled past Allen's Shoes at 324 W Main St. in August 1938.

The post office installed lighted signs in November 1934 to guide patrons to "Stamps," "COD Delivery," "Claims," "Parcel Post" and other windows. Loraine Patrick and Mabel Hunt were happy to show *The Daily Oklahoman's* photographer the difference between the new, lighted sign and the old, unlighted "Mail Drops" version it succeeded.

## Busy streets

Constructed in 1902, the Culbertson Building, center in photograph at left, looked as if it sat in the middle of Broadway. Instead, it marked the spot where different surveying crews, one north of Grand and the other south, had come up with different opinions about sizes of city blocks and their alignment. The view was to the south.

The Oklahoma City branch of the Federal Reserve Bank of Kansas City opened in 1920 at Second Street and Broadway, and three years later moved to its own new building at Harvey and Third streets, above. Its employees processed checks from most Oklahoma banks. Inside, the vault was guarded by a 100,000-pound door, reputed to be the largest and thickest west of the Mississippi at the time.

Right: A new traffic signal installed downtown in 1929 used only lights and dispensed with the semaphore of earlier models. Seventeen more were to be placed at various intersections.

The latest look in drugstores, 1938: Interior of the new Walgreen's at Main Street and Harvey Avenue. The chain had about 500 stores nationwide at the time.

The American National Bank building in the 1910s, not long after it was constructed.

When the new Oklahoma County courthouse in the Civic Center opened in 1937, its predecessor, right, sat empty for several years. The old courthouse was built in 1904-1906 at 520 W Main St. in a style called "massive Romanesque."

The Patterson Building on Main Street boasted the city's most elaborate terra cotta façade, topped by cast-iron beacon lighting fixtures. Inside, it had two-inch-thick marble slabs and a central vacuuming system. It was built by L.E. Patterson, a developer and early streetcar owner. By 1938, when this photograph was made, the structure bore the name "Equity Building."

## Christmastime in the city

Beginning in the 1920s, Oklahoma City's downtown merchants dressed up the streets holiday-style with multicolored lights, wreaths and garlands. Left to right from facing page: the nighttime scene in 1936; busy sidewalks in 1935; pupils at a school classroom decoration in 1929.

Left: In the 1920s, *The Daily Oklahoman* conducted a home lighting contest. The W.R. Ramsey mansion on W 16 Street won the 1929 prize in its geographical section of the city and the category of homes costing more than $7,500.

Crowds jammed the sidewalks, left, along Main Street in 1934, many rushing home with their treasures. The Mid-Continent Life Insurance Company building at 13 Street and Classen Boulevard, above, showed off its lights in 1929. Right: A street scene from, 1935.

## Whims of weather

Destructive, discouraging and difficult to predict: The weather in Oklahoma. On June 9, 1937, three tornadoes swept across central Oklahoma, one of them smashing this house south of Oklahoma City, above. The owners, who were tossed from their home by the storm, were hospitalized in critical condition at Oklahoma City General. In all the storms, one person died and 13 were hurt.

Right: When a snowstorm bore down on the state in early January 1940, the city deployed about 250 unemployed men to clear sidewalks downtown. Each man received $1 for the day's work, half from the city and half from the county.

## The eve of conflict

War lay thousands of miles away across the oceans in 1941, but radio and newspapers kept it in the minds of most Americans. Evidence of the European conflict was beginning to be seen in Oklahoma City, where in February 1941 members of a British purchasing commission clambered on a pile of scrap iron for use in their war effort. A bloc of Americans, however, distrusted the British and opposed U.S. aid to that country. Among them was aviator Charles Lindbergh, who visited Oklahoma City in late October 1941 to speak at the invitation of the state America First Committee. Its chairman, Herbert K. Hyde, greeted Lindbergh at the airport, above left. At Sandlot baseball park, Lindbergh joined former governor "Alfalfa Bill" Murray and Hyde to say that an air war between the United States and Germany would end in a standoff. Britain, he warned, might turn on America if the United States entered the conflict. Murray, for years a foe of President Roosevelt and the New Deal, condemned the administration's "duplicity."

The pro-British side matched Lindbergh's celebrity by bringing in Gene Autry, the nationally famous singing cowboy and movie star who also owned a ranch in Oklahoma. He was welcomed at the airport by Governor Leon C. Phillips, above. A crowd estimated at 8,500 jammed Municipal Auditorium to hear Autry sing, "I'm Back in the Saddle Again" and "Tumbling Tumbleweed." He urged the audience to buy defense stamps and bonds and sang one song that hinted at scorn for the "America First" adherents: "If you don't like your Uncle Sam … don't bite the hand that's feeding you."

A vigorous advocate of aid to the British, Senator Claude Pepper, left, of Florida also visited Oklahoma City in 1941.

Above: While the debate raged, the military draft already was taking young Oklahomans into the service. Private Bouton Brown, 23, of Oklahoma City was one whose name was drawn in the lottery in October 1940, a preparatory measure for the United States. Brown, like many others, was assigned to Fort Sill and hoped to be out of the Army by Christmas 1941 — unless the United States went to war. In early December 1941, the United States would do just that.

# Index

All photographs are from the Oklahoma Publishing Company Collection of the Oklahoma Historical Society. Thousands more can be seen at the society's Gateway to Oklahoma History website, **https://gateway.okhistory.org/**